whorelight

Linda Ashok

Hawakal Publishers

whorelight

Published by Subhra Chakraborty
on behalf of Hawakal Publishers

185, Kali Temple Road, Nimta, Calcutta
700049, India.

Website: www.hawakal.com
Contact: info@hawakal.com

Copyright: Linda Ashok
First edition (Paperback): August, 2017
Printed and bound at S. P. Communications, Calcutta.

Cover concept: Linda Ashok
Designed by chitrangi

ISBN-13: 978-8193423080

Price: INR 225/- / US Dollar 9.99

Dadu

FOREWORD

The borderland between the sensory, the remembered, and the imagined is peopled with dreams, not just the dreams we have at night but the dreams implicit in language where several worlds often blend into one. Language, we say, is organized, systematic, safely lodged in dictionaries, but dictionaries are never as secure as we imagine them at the point of exchange or in the shops of everyday life where a tin of beans always means a tin of beans not a ton of bones.

In literature we may choose to call our dream transactions something like Surrealism or Magic Realism but our names for such things are no more secure than our names for what we feel or think or even say. Language is nothing without system, but no system is reality.

Poetry moves between the cracks in the system. It is the fresh water beneath the parched soil of language. We can navigate surfaces but the soil produces nothing out of depth without it. Without it we cannot recognize the world we ourselves experience and continue to experience at depth.

Linda's poetry is particularly agile in shifting between the cracks in search of precise fresh feeling. Those shifts are the product of reflections on feelings already known, on ways of exploring new feelings produced by the old ones, and on the suggestive power of language itself.

The poems typically start from an unnamed but intense emotion then run through a series of associations, each of which is rooted in something sensory. The basic terms can be grand, romantic and universal as in "Promises We Make," the very first poem in the book that refers to moons and stars, and heaven and planets, while invoking fireflies and a lighthouse. It's a dash between the great and the small, the universal and the specific.

Her attention is not entirely subjective or locked within the self and its dramas, but is constantly looking out at, for example:

> *...the lives of workers*
> *inked by the grime of disquiet machines*
> *and trees berried wild and luscious*
> *in which the workers noted their sunsets*
> *and counted wages...* "The First Time"

The language here is as luscious as the berries that are associated with "*the grime of disquiet machines*" (her use of language is sometimes unorthodox, slipping sideways). She often perceives a latent violence in things:

> *Her head opened up*
> *like a can of coke...* "Portrait of Guilt"

Frequently the poems are addressed to specific people in the tones of an intimate, urgent conversation. Occasionally the speaker is someone else, like the speaker of "Wheel Chair." This is not a purely subjective world. Politics is alluded to by its effects. Sometimes it feels almost like reportage:

> *All dead men, wilted lotus stems,*
> *tied and bundled, bullet holes repaired.*
> *Men on this side of the border receive*
> *them, sign the papers, and vice versa.* "Apropos"

But it's never pure reportage. Mostly it's that fast moving set of intense feelings surging between the cracks, seeking a shape. The body and the sensations of the body play a vital part in this. In one of the many prose poems of the collection, "You Ask If This Is Love," she starts with the body and shifts to parallel images before slipping back:

> *At this hour of the day, I am making love to*
> *a body that has left home long time before the*
> *rain began. It is empty inside...*
>
> *...I walk in and watch the bones disappear*
> *into smoke and building walls on which no*
> *birds can ever come to rest.*

At other times, as in "An Exit Morphs Our Flesh," the process is reversed:

We are set for the journey; houses look soft after days of rain... The road is a clean tongue covering our bodies in shining asphalt. We walk naked for miles until birds and animals and other kindred spirits find their ways through us and we become the path to passing time...

To whom should we compare Linda Ashok? It is hard to pick any particular poet because she shares a kinship with many and yet she is fully herself, a poet in development but one of great energy and singular promise. Her voice and vision are fresh, energizing the reader who is willing to move with her and be refreshed by that movement, her energy always seeking the control necessary to realise that energy and give it its full power as if by a careless grace, a grace, that at her best, she does indeed achieve without apparently trying. It is fresh water.

George Szirtes
July 14, 2017
England, United Kingdom

CONTENTS

PROMISES WE MAKE

For A.B

I'll send you over the moon, and you'll break the stars
and bring to my dark body the milk of heaven.

I'll send you over the planets, and you can read
to the cosmos stories of our bodies dumbfound,
dead, after a night long laceration of the waves.

I'll send fireflies to the lighthouse to be able
to signal the world that you aren't alone
and your flesh will soon be phosphorescence,
eaten by me, bemused.

I heard you. Read all the messages.
Then marked them unread so you think
and still hope for my response some day
when I am around. I am already in it.
I just do not want to tell you that I am
waiting, waiting for the musk in your belly
to press against mine and squash the pods
and release the dizzy essence of belonging.

I have heard you. Just waiting for your
battle to be over to begin a new one where
I'll be your candy and you, my rogue.

HOW TO NEAR LOVE AND NOT BE ASKING

After Mary Howe

When the long fingers of our coconut tree
knock on the window to remind it is morning,
I am already awake trying to convince the mind
that sometimes genes can make an exception.

—childless at thirty, is not becoming
 of a woman, get her a hormone check, many
women are lesbians, they don't let their eggs
                    to the kind men, an aunty once said—

But I am thirty, just finished paying my debts.
It is time, you should be a mother, said
my homemaker girlfriends.

I look at a fledgling in the nest or a cub
in the manger, I look at an insect nursing her
kind or a woman breastfeeding her newborn,
I feel an ache and the skin on my body
falls like a garment loosely stitched,
worn out through inconsiderate rubs.

The coconut tree too, laughs at me
showing off her tender water babies.

Being thirty, dreading a turnaround of life
against the scarlet throes disposed in the genes,
nearing every lover as a hopeless woman
wanting a child, are things

no good woman should suffer—
consult a yogi, said another aunty.

WHEN YOU TALK ABOUT A DEAD DEER

For Kelli Russel Agodon

The buds in my garden respond to such grief with a
refusal to open up their petals in full light. Air, dank
with sorrow, makes my garden smell like a cemetery.
Ghosts juggle in the bath under feet and I can only
hear a trombone, a devastating note grafted by the
wind on my broken cello still living with a heart and
two kidneys. The flowers in my garden (once a forest,
till my last lover set a tomb here to beat the snow and
reach the last breath with as less anguish for death
possible) were untamable; they chased the deer and the
lost alike. The lost dropped one by one, so did the
deer. Grief stilled their bloom until my wild hands
relieved them of the guilt and they became tamer.
When you talk about a dead deer, it reminds me of the
builder of my nest who sailed tons of musk pods
down the Yangtse to a bustling metropolis and
wondered how someone's horror, someone's pain can
be sold for money. He then died here, in redemption,
and in his body was impermanence sculpted of regret,
of a lifetime measured in dead deer.

CLOTS

Crossing a blue trail of overhead litter, I come to a festival of poets and sit inside the womb of Mary waiting for Christ to take the stage and sing for his father (now out, on vent). He asks for prayers and walls open their pores to breathe out memories, to make room for new energies bursting at the spire. Everyone, I suppose, has known a clot; sometimes dangerous, sometimes sweet and vulnerable, ready to shed petals and suck the stillness of the roads now retired from their homes.

Running in the morning light trying to catch the falling tide I gather your voice in my shoes and wear them back to where I begin writing this poem too shy to confess how it notices countries walking naked through your face and people too happy to go on a walk with animal dreams on their tongues. My feet, wet and luminous. My nails, little glass screens offering a preview of the undersea, of debris forming new structures.

I ask what happened to your poem? You say my poem is doing a lot better. There were clots in his head but we hope the operation will restore him to page. I pause in memory of a clot that once stayed too long till I cut an exit and tattooed a fern. Now I move to the station bridge in Hove, where under a chandelier of clots, a man counts the changes before settling inside a giant violin case. No one around. Not even a gull. In my mind, that baby fox I met on my way and then, this cold violin that pulls a lull over her master's sleeping body...

I leave a pound, then retract, and find my way down the running throat of space. Next day, I wake up with the sun in my lungs, once again burning images into perfect clots.

Note: "Running in the morning light trying to catch the falling tide" Disraeli

THE FIRST TIME

When he asked her
to get up,

she was contemplating
on the lives of workers

inked by the grime
of disquiet machines

and trees berried
wild and luscious

in which the workers
noted their sunsets

and counted wages.
He asked her to get up-

"There is a gift for you,"
he said. Then he shut

the window
and the workers

morphed from dizzy
berries to restricted entries.

And while the butterflies rallied
out of the deceased factory,

he broke the glass & rubbed
her lips with molten scar.

PORTRAIT OF GUILT

That night,
I dreamt of a woman
in *salwar kameez*
falling off from the backseat
of a speeding car.

Her head opened up
like a can of coke.
Women pruning grass
on the kerb
held her face as if
a broken flower pot
and dumped her
in the carrion-box.

You were not
a part of this dream.
I was alone in the backseat
imagining a hand
across my shoulder
vaguely smelling
of the shirt
you wore to the forest.

WHEEL CHAIR

For Arka Datta

Listen, I do have legs, just that I have to get the writing done. These women who promised to stay put, their memories, I guess have new calls to answer. Anyway, pass me the salt and tell me if cooking experienced the ages that all our literature went through. You know, the first woman, she did have a strange take on caviar—she called them shingles of post-modernity. That had me. She came to my bed, as if to love, my penis thankful already, but we went into discussing the directorial tricks of her Korean boyfriend.

And then the other: The other woman sold me all her flowers because I was smitten by the poster girl in purple lingerie right across her shoulder. She thought I was reading her eyes. This repeated until one day I went to her shop in my wheelchair and she held my hands and we made treacherous love behind the shacks. It was just that her boyfriend threatened to break my legs and dump me in a tank of sharks that I step back. The knowledge about sixteen varieties of roses, the cap on her molar, and her sweet tongue...

Oh well, the art school teacher was different. She loved my globe feet and her fetish found a new admiration. Being naked, with blades of sun sparingly shading my body, she wanted my legs crossed and feet visible for that summer of paintings which went on for successful sales. She bought me fruits and stories of her son studying medicine in Damascus.

Thanks for the salt. But you should know, I do not mean to discourage our love. I just mean, I do have legs, but I trust the wheels.

APROPOS

All dead men; wilted lotus stems,
tied and bundled, bullet holes repaired.
Men on this side of the border receive
them, sign the papers, and vice versa.
Poor farmers refuse but then convinced that
these will decompose and offer good wheat.

You ask for a massage of your stiff shoulders.
The cat hears those stems calling her away.
I try not to give her a listen and open the letter
in which you talk about tendons and snow cuffs,
you talk about our last kiss, and how the boat
broke and we faltered in the water, and yet…

I didn't expect you at the door so soon.
I know, however, you had to flee countries
and so you brought me here to watch our
neighbor return the wilted men packed with
no visible dents. Sometimes, the cat and I
congeal and it says, "Now, you are wheat!"

CHILLI FLAKES

Why did you run away?
You could trust the government
It is not like North Korea
Your women still sing and dance.
Your men still care if babies
have runny noses
or stay with the family
if your city wears a curfew
Look, this is how you put
the batter into the oven. Just
ensure the cheese is evenly
spread so that the crust is well
set and moist.   Now tell me,
why did you run away? I am
sure it is not just because of me.
Ahh! Pass me the chilli flakes.
I missed it.

MARK IT WITH *F*

No, but we will live a life together, by the sea. You will bake breads, and I'll raise your child and tell her that she is not born of refugee fund but of that delicious stuffing from the scone of our lives.

\#

One day, you'll buy a carpet and a new porcelain vase for flowers to welcome me home after hours in the labor. Your hands hard from kneading dough for extra-hours, you'll miss your mother. You will step back and call her name aloud. But she won't be around for you.

\#

I'll ask you your reason for sorrow and you will say, "Men are never sorry. Men don't cry." I will believe you so that you are not hurt. You'll explain the politics of Brexit and how France should file a divorce. You'll know that divorce is not my favorite word, so you'll touch my baby bump and promise to always stay together, even in fights.

\#

It'll rain outside. You'll try to recall your idea of rain. I'll talk about floods. You'll say how I am being funny, and with the midwife, you'll ask me to hold my breath. I'll; .hold and release my body and let the world out in your hands. You'll look into her eyes and say, "France...nay, Francine is born."

LETTER TO THE BUNION TOE MAN

a door cut out of fresh morning air/ three poets, a painter, and a hippie gone mellow/ in your mind, two boys gathering berries, your twelve-year olds/ a transcriptionist setting dishes out for wash.../ notwithstanding a few anthills/ eavesdropping our silences

"every time, my hand rose by the side/ the bamboo paused me in bizarre ways/ you stood still at the corner and later, on the beanbag/ with no hunch of attempts"

two forests meet for a while, sing to each other/ exchange birds, chaos, and merge, not forgetting the wood/ they carry back to their idea of homes

we will die in this silence, like the bone/ in your toe that never complains, still dying

INSIDE THE HEAD OF A TREE

is a toy
for lovers
to breathe clean

and shed their skins
and turn their bones

into branches
into tapes

to record
what the diplomats
won't reveal otherwise

about the pattern
of a great crumble.

Take that toy
and come to it
open mouth.

Wear that skull
of mirror and walk.

When tired,
ask for light and I'll come

with suns burning my hands.

BLOOD PAISLEYS

Some wounds ooze light, and it is at dawn
the peonies raise their heads to receive the day
outside my room, through the wound I see her
emerging like a cecropia moth soaping her wings.

I can feel a wave choking the lighthouse—her
body a minaret smoking early morning fog.
Hesitatingly, I leave my bed and remove the curtain
from the wound, set aside the peonies, and drink

from her breath—her paisley breasts carry the weight
of a childhood lost in some village, of youth sold
by a beloved to an urban household to do the dishes.
I am here for a while, in the bath, her body too…

MANY LIVES OF A MEMORY

In the middle of baking,
I forget that memory
is biodegradable,
that it blends
with the berries
in the soil,
in the scum

under feet.
I forget not to let
memory be under the oak.

It quacks, a nestling
its mother gone
for baking bread
to feed the topaz void.

I pull the caramel,
dice the apples
I pull, I dice
but forget the names

that memory, once.
gave to each.

In the verandah,
the bicycle naps

beside the petunias
that smell of rose

But roses, they are-
he exclaims on the phone.

I started with the batter,
lost all ingredients.
Now counting a few gondolas
feasting in my arteries.

ON YOUR BIRTHDAY

For Saikat Sarkar

Remove the curtains. Watch those little oceans wanting to fly away and feel the world with wings you gave to him at birth. See how those two oceans on his face blink.

Then turn to the woman, talk to her about windmills you have never seen but you must.

Talk to her about the lather on her skin that you fancy when her baby has skipped her bosom, and she is tender and spring.

Then turn around at yourself, and take a look at the memories you shelved for ages and how time glazes them with a baroque finish. Hear them bless you and move away.

It is now time to go—wish for rain secretly, and have the road welcome you to a new walk. You don't need birthday songs but the opening of a few new tulips.

BECOMING A RICE POT

She held the rice pot too
close to her bosom each time
she had to take a cup of it.
Once she would take as
much, she would keep back
a fistful. She never wanted
the rice pot to be empty.
Keeping back, she told me
years later, is restraint. When
you make a good home,
remember, holding back
a little every time will
save you the magic.
When he called me last
summer, I wanted to hold
back a little of myself, but
a sudden gust of *Kalbaisakhi*
changed the conversation.

OF WATERS, MANNERS

the waters return home
play with boats, dead sea-men, shells

and when done, they bring back
the toys to where their burial belong

...the way pain returns us our bones
or a gazelle forgives her hunter...

the waters return everything
except time and its own iridescence

THE UNMAKING OF AN ASTRONAUT

I.
i count the change as you draw closer
>your shirt smelling of God's own sweat

i roll you up in a lane leading to my budget space
the lacquer on your tongue, your nails following my
steps.

the metro is indistinct in the morning smog. it isn't
the monorail. i wish I could remove the window
and have the geraniums nap in the rain

but you pull the curtain... take the roof away
defy gravity and thrust skyward

i careen in the air

asking for blackness
asking for water
asking more of you

II.
another day:

your skin almost as thick as light;
an aquarium—in it,

a girl with a bowl of dead moths

traversing a space built of snow, trying to bury them

III.
yet another day:

silence manifests itself
in a plate of rice and *tandoori*

i paint the wall: an ocean, you offer the mast;
we become the hull.

DIRTY LOVE

A beach is a pretty place to kiss
but I don't want to kiss you at pretty places

I want to kiss you under the bed
on the bathroom pot
while washing your wearables
while on the wait for your train
at the station, at taxi stands

I want to kiss you by the masjid
by the tea-stall, house of the congress
and the conservatives
I want to kiss you in a public toilet

and places that are not as pretty as the beach

Because:
  i.   I only know how to make dirty love &
  ii.   My absence can only love you as much

TREE INSPECTOR

He: These trees will take time to grow. Do not worry. So? Are you from India?

She: [*Nods her head in assent.*] What about you?

He: I am from Maine, in Berkshire for two years. I live by the farm across the highway in a little cottage left behind by my father's third wife who had eyes as big as yours. You know about trees? My father, while in the asylum, planted trees for each inmate who needed someone to believe in their stories. But they didn't let my father live long. They convicted him for treason and when all the tests failed, they felled him too and all those that he had planted. I ran away with his book of seeds.

She: [*Breathes, looks around, breathes and listens again.*]

He: Does India have too many trees? I know, like many you are not likely to believe my story, and so, I share them with the trees. When I am gone, and these trees grow up, you can ask them my name. I'll be in the rounds. You can call me for tea.

CATCHING UP

"Most of the time I walk
alone and pick up the lost streams
on my way and place them
back to where they belong,"
said the old man by the mountains
out in the moon with his shadow.

"Tired and exhausted, my eyes
lovingly take the memories of trees
and plant them in the desert
for camels to find home
in the scorching language of summer."
I ask him for guidance.

He exhales birds to fill the branches
and with the passing of the day,
his heart loses its shape.
Thick moonlight on my father's brush
tries to bury his broken past;
those branches in full bloom now.

He still bends forward, guards
the seeds from being carried away.
His shadow, scared, woofs.
They break and rebound (*love
lost many times, yet the hourglass's
wait for the sand to fill her up*).

WHEN HE COMES BACK

When he comes back, I cross
the two thin ribbons of light
that the sun and trees play
with and I think of Van Gogh
striking off our memories.

Cars may hit me.
Shadow may pull off my body

leaving my bones for the gulls
to peck at the residue of longing
that has traced my nerves into a rich
upholstery to be cremated with care.

His voice like branches
spring like a fountain with birds
ringing in every branch.

A windchime, I, do not heed
to the world colliding in wars,
arguments, and injuries

The road opens up infinite possibilities
propelling my wings from falling,

from reaching home.

MIRROR

I love listening to you talking about trees
and guessing the kind of bird by the sound
of her wings. You say it is an art of a canvas
leaving her colors and brushes as bouquets
to her painter.

Many a time, you know, I just wanted
to keep quiet and let the morning light spider
me love that I feel when I hear you talking
to the trees and meditate on their wisdom
that runs light years deep.

Tell me, did a canvas ever refuse you, have you
been isolated in an island of birds, have you
ever walked strange countries and taken aback
by stories of your homeland on sale?

How did you feel? Did you walk up to them?
Did you hear if they spoke the language that
the bird left in your tongue? How did you feel
being auctioned not in person, but in grief?

Many a time, you know, I love listening
to you, I love seeing you naked and take
pride in this belonging. So that if a sudden
impulse handcuffs my life, you would know
that a peace-treaty is already signed.

A CALM THAT RIDES ME

I bring the lamp to the soft glow of your skin. Veins empty into petals. Outside, snow covers that garden like a cat covering her shit. I imagine this is no extraordinary dusk swallowing me like the oven gets drunk on fevered gas. Do you feel the rust in the air? The sky's got mold and it'll break indefinitely till our shoes are lost in one leg. In front of me, the brown skirt that knows your hands, your aversion to waters, and its strange intuition of our becoming. Good days are seizures dispossessing the owner of this calm; the calm that labors to treat me to an origami sleep. Wish you were here to put hands into one skin and press the eyes into one view. So colorless, yet the taste of winter on coarse moonlight...

INSIDE A POEM IS A WORM

thinking of people
as riotous gods—

possessed,
their tongues beetroot

their bodies, canals
of debris flushed down

the sinks
that fracture minds

into lands thirsted
by birds for ages before

the farmers had to stop
thinking of rice

and wear hungry bellies
in rib freezing nights.

Inside this poem,
is a worm that fears

abundance.

UNTONGUE

At this moment,
if there is anything that a poem
can talk about is the proximity

that binds us in utter falseness.
And then rain that fills up the puddles
for ants to cross the channel
rowing a shadow of palm leaf.

Poems are dangerous.
Like babies. They absorb
from shit to sorrow to sobriety.
So, be careful when you speak.

Be careful
when you advance
to un-tongue me.

WINDOW, EN-SUITE

My Chinese neighbor next door, a young man
opens his window and looks through the bare

branches of the trees awaiting sun. He pulls
out the flower vases from his lungs

and fills them up with mist to soothe
the ruby shingles at the joints of his nerves.

He does not smoke and warns me
of the suffering of his sister who laughs

like cotton balls on the face of wars.
I can imagine, or you can say, too frequently

visited by the idea of failing to catch the train
to somewhere safe, to..., I guess mortality?

but then we have to die, die like those weaver
birds, like those many stars dying in silence,

of creature born of mud and blood, who by pain
or by luck, has found a home in the thin air

that cuts sharp like butterfly wings slicing
spring into memorious halves, giving them

back to the cherry blossoms, or daffodils

giving them back to the rodents to finish a cycle.

My Chinese neighbor, on unemployment benefit,
remembers his deceased father killed in Yarlong
Tsangpo.

CHANDRANI

I

She had a collection of wild plumes. She had killed
many birds and kept their hearts in her box of jewels.
Many a times when she cried for her three year old
who she had to leave in the custody of her husband
over a *triple talaq*, she would rise like *maya*, rub her lips
scathing red, wear her local Victoria, tuck all feathers,
and pirouette like a sufi till that little grief had broken
her ribs. [You hear: You hear the gentle sway, the
swish of a falling leaf.]

All the while, I would lie down, watch her body spin,
her plumes afire. I would feel love, turn over, and
write poems.

II

In the evenings when Chandrani will sit and watch my
father paint, I would imagine her in many ways.

She was my sister aborted, my step mother abused, my
mother abandoned ... She was the perfect body I
desired to wear, a sister to love and a stranger woman
to sleep with counting how many bones make a fish
swim. The day we both had to leave for office the
same time, and landlord had warned about water being
available for half an hour, we turned in naked for bath.
[You see: Water from our mugs splashing each other's
backs.] [You don't see: a lizard bites the moth hard in
her heart.]

PROCESSING THE ORDER

Have you been unkind to sorrow,
knelt before the sun for too long
asking him to shine harder on you?
Have you closed the little wooden gate
of your heart to prevent sorrow from ravaging
the shelf of your high worth and low?
Sorrow is a deaf child with clipped wings.
Sorrow is blind, soaked red beans.
Trust me, they understand
that you fear, that a sponge too
over a period of inattention becomes
rock that the poor can build their homes with.
It is okay to be the underlying, them agrees.
It is also okay to cage them,
light fragrant candles and give
all of yourself to someone else,
to something else.
Sorrow survives every reason,
every joy, periods that redden the skies
even if you have shut the door on them.
It'll stay with you the way
a dog kennels inside a God.

WHORE

I have seen a woman
by the edge of the country
where the river enters
without a passport
in broad daylight
and the army lets her in
because guns are for those
who know guns.

The river is the friend,
of the woman who sits there
with a sewing machine hoping
to see her son come back.
While she's at work, the river
shares with her, the count
of men dumped in her lap.

"Whore," they call her, for she
has given herself to all weathers
alike. There, she sits at her sewing machine
running meters of skin with fireflies
and cicadas so that the spirits of people
sold for labor across the border
do not feel loveless.

She bottles frost and fear,
risk and rain and gives them away

to men, hoping the news of her son
will take her home, wrap
in a shroud and lay her down
in her frostbitten grave.

EARLY LESSONS IN VIOLENCE

My first lesson in violence was tearing the terminal abdomen of a dragonfly and shoving it up with grass. Hunger visited us often times and like an old uncle pervert in his means of touching the body, hunger found its way to our bed even in the middle of night when the garden tomatoes would give in to the appetite of worms and the voyeur moon would play her cello.

Grandfather's pension would mean some lamb roasted in coal and potato halves glazed with mustard. But what I enjoyed more than the food was the killing itself; the way men of our village brought home their kill—women sold to them with cattle or lambs of good breed. Because when lust would leave the last station the track would be an old dirge smelling of blood.

Father worked in a lead factory, a thousand bullets a day to earn a living. But despite that, I stole them everytime, loaded his gun, and killed bats that hung like ridiculous fruits. I hated them chirping. I envied their little stomach always full to the brim unlike a pariah that could never eat her kill alone. The bats I killed, every day, I would bring them home, take the pips out, and suck their sweet flesh like violence would.

PARABLE OF A SOMNAMBULIST

Last night, as I was ready to pull the blanket on myself, I heard mother sleep talking. A sea-spirit at the bank of a river with a huge fishnet caught mother in its spell. Mother was asking for help but I pulled the blanket over my ears and just left my eyes open to her like our bedroom window keeps her eyes open to the street below visited by random dreams on feet or bikes. Mother kept her hands on her breasts and that is why the spirit could smell her heart. I went back to those days in childhood when mother would sit up for hours trying to recover me from a dream as cunning as crocodiles pouncing on zebras on National Geographic. For long, I fancied interpreting the borealis of the human mind, but Freud kind of said that I'll be more inclined to help if it is father in trouble. So, I stayed still, watched her iridescent speech morph into groans, brave the waves, and then let her wild whale take the spirit by its ribs and rip it into shreds. I made no move. All I was concerned of was my cold feet which I placed on her legs. Mother, then turned around and kissed me on the forehead. "Sleep," she said, "I have killed the ghost."

RUINS WITH PERFECT EYES LIKE YOURS

For A.B

Every time it would rain, the ashes of my village would transmute into pretty animals and as usual, all, all of them will also have wings; pale, membranous wings almost the color of your eyes; eyes that have sown the seeds of rain in my body, now nothing less than a forest where the animals of my village spring in joy and mate eternally for many ruins with perfect eyes like yours to be born. Only on cold days like this, the forest dies emptying its chorus, surrendering itself to the weight of a seed of rain. Everything is like never before, once again.

KILLING MOTHS

Cold is a beautiful touch;
her eyes are cold, resplendent—
centuries old fossils clawing for light.

She is like an aquarium;
you can see how avalanches
can make one so soft…
If you place your hands inside
her glassy, gelatinous body,
you can save yourself a frostbite.

Last month, I dyed her hair
with moonbeam… and pitched a moth
in each crevice of her braid.
While I did so, I enjoyed killing them
and dirtying her brown nape with its dust.

YOU ASK IF THIS IS LOVE

For A.B

At this hour of the day, I am making love to a body that has left home long time before the rain began. It is empty inside. The skies have lent me a few eyes that hover in that darkness like fireflies remembering hard their addresses. I tip toe on my breath lest this country wakes up and labels me a mad woman who lost her limbs and jaws in grief that was smaller than the size of his fist. I walk in and watch the bones disappear into smoke and building walls on which no birds can ever come to rest. You ask, if this is love? I close the door and let the song take me in its weave. How gentle it is to be woven into a woolen waiting to steal the grace of winter. I am making love, I insist, only your face is missing!

TO RUN WITH AN EMPTY NEST

It isn't a pretty thing to do
but I was only trying to stay away
from this spring that comes
with birds and blossoms
reminding me
of something
they took out
from one half
of an hourglass.

Here's the thing—

I can sit with emptiness,
talk to her about the empty
church corridors,
talk to her about the aftermath
of a meteor shower, or stillness
that pays the last visit
to a victim
of a road accident

But in no way can I stop spring
to remind a part of me
they flushed down the sink.

WAITING

A little wound floats
above the dark waters
I hold its shadow up
like an umbrella and walk
in my vanishing suit
O passing wind, just look
at me for once and lift me up
Cut a window in my eyes
I want to see the valley of fallen
stars, of white honeycombs
and doppelgangers
ferrying dreams of choice
or just throw me like
a bobbin in the air
and let the rivers
trapped in this flesh break
This waiting is a sea wasp
Its poison bubbles inside...

HYMN FOR THE MAN BY PERIYAR

this thick yarn of emptiness
is all I have to feel warm
in your absence
this rudimentary landscape
your cold, shining jaws
and a janitor called moment
drug me to sleepless hours
and endless trek
through nothingness

when the moon spills over Periyar,
don't drown yourself

This love is not safe.

HOW CAN I SAY I DREAMT OF YOU

For A.B

Until I woke up, it was all easy for me. I knew I could talk about it. I could tell you how exactly the tap had become a cobra and took our hands and swallowed them to never return the love that was blurring the palm-lines. Until I woke up, I knew I could convince you that we are good without them, that we can still sow seeds with our mouths, etch the soil, spit the seeds and wait for life to surprise us with flowers that would be poisonous to anyone touching them with envy. I was sure I could tell you that even when the soil refused to accept our bodies without hands and legs eaten by the courtyard mist hungry for ages, even without our eyes that flew away to cover for the fruitless old tree that never saw a bird... We were happy becoming a clump of decay but now that I woke up, I have lost all evidences and I can't say, trust me, in fancy we were one.

AN EXIT MORPHS OUR FLESH

For A.B

We are set for the journey; houses look soft after days of rain... The road is a clean tongue covering our bodies in shining asphalt. We walk naked for miles until birds and animals and other kindred spirits find their ways through us and we become the path to passing time. There is no rage, no race, no countries moaning our departure. In your lungs, songs play that steadily drip from memories you crafted to gift me a pair of crystal eyes in which light breaks its prism into many hues without dropping a clue. For, the very first time that I have seen you gleaming in love is when an exit morphs our flesh to sand.

VOICE TO A WINGLESS CREATURE

For A.B

There is so much in your voice; for one moment I think of it as the house that lay broken in my memory, for the other, it is sea-salt tediously saving itself from the mouth of an ocean... This is the voice where birds are mechanically passed into the grinder and rolled into meatballs. This voice is a handmade mirror where my face breaks into several pieces and I tidily pick up each shard to rearrange it again. Sorry, it is your voice but I feel a tremor in my lungs as you pronounce each word smelling of petrichor, smelling like the leftover of memories that have made me a mess of nothingness. Your voice, a crevice and I, a wingless creature, thrust by the violent wind...

ABSENCE SETS IN LIKE RIGOR MORTIS

I have cut this winter evening into a lantern to take you through the snow of my mind. Hold it gently and let the fire not burn you down but only keep you as warm enough to be able to accept the receipt of wounds for healing is erasing the circus you choreographed and you wish I do not...

I know you are far away, tearing birds and feeding the hunger that's gradually leaving your body.

Age, you see? Even birds don't seem to satisfy what was once covered by love walking the edges of the earth trying to measure how many meters of light can cover the darkness of your heart.

"Youth is a bastard," you said, "It will save you from longing, from shoe bites, from hunger itself." But now, I am sure it's been many ages since war has shown you a firefly aching on its back at which you remarked, "Poor one, it's not here to die but masturbate its absence and pass on the fire."

WINTER MUSK

It is winter. The lakes around my house talk to the musk deer. The other day, she was wounded, heavily bleeding. When she tried to gauge the depth of her wound, the wind took her face away. She looked from inside and she looked hard until her face started to appear from the mouth of her wound. Now she has two faces. The one returned by the wind and the one that grew in the wound. She can now switch between the sad and the happy faces. She has a face for the humans and she has a face for the lakes. It is winter. The lakes breathe her incense.

A THOUSAND DEAD MOTHS

Sometimes feeling love is such a personal thing that you want to be by yourself, dangling your legs down a French window of a skyscraper, feel the wind rise inside your body and waves break and leave you wanting, gasping, terrorized for that little touch that may forever be a figment, eluding you. To feel love, you have to pull yourself out of the envelop that God posted in a side way postbox of an abandoned mountain village where chill confines berries to the moist tongue of soil... Unfold, like you step out of the coffin that is not yet ready to push beyond its means and lift yourself in silent admiration of the quietness that fills your body, digs a tunnel and blows in a thousand dead moths with intimacy marked on their chests.

GLASS KIDS OF FIROZABAD

I once told a woman
wearing shiny glass bangles

that she looked scary. She turned
at me curious and offended.

She was eager to know and I, eager to show-
On one hand, I traced a sad boy's face

and on the other, I unearthed a girl
almost dead, with one eye pushed deep
into the socket and stitched.

Terrified, she looked at her husband
She took off all those bangles

And as they broke, they released
the spirits of glass kids

One bangle wheeled across
the road at the feet of an old lady

throwing balls for her pup to catch.

SOUGH

For A.B

The sun is often unscrupulous. See the curtains on my window are wet with its fire and you call it light. I would say it is the same darkness with which you wash your mouth and clean the dishes. I know you will not agree because businesses believe in the packaging, and I am talking about content of a radical, genuine self that dissects a dog to bring out its heart and understand loyalty as some organic pus. Listen, take your hands away from the curtain, else its fire may calcify your bones and call it development. I don't want to see how you look from inside because the insides as you say are most redundant, and hence the packaging. But please, do come, sit by this run and deposit of time, say something nice so that the darkness cleaved between my breasts can set itself free. If you press your ears deep in this moment, you will hear the soughing. In that you and I and everything around us are waves speeding toward an ending so grossly splendid, so neatly tough, yet inviting. Unscrupulous if you call it, let's be clouds and hold within this yolk of living, until a thunder cracks us open and we spill, like lovers, like rain on parched metal.

GIFT

A neckpiece
of sugared fireflies

A lighthouse
full of wrecks

A sea wasp
that obeys touch

A yarn
of sinking

And distance
that keeps us together

DECAY

When God was tidying his room, a crow came in with a fish rib and dipped it in tar kept in a tin on the window sill. God asked what that is, and she cawed, "An exercise to prevent the decay of the passing world." Nonplussed, he looked around in search of something and walked away.

Since then, the crow brought many ribs from the ocean, from the graves, and bleeding cities. She dipped them in tar and arranged them on the sill to dry until one day, God returned with what he was looking for. He gave the crow a bone from his rib and asked, "Can this be treated to prevent the decay of the world?"

TONGUE TIED

How deep is the universe? How many
light years will it take to reach your belly

by way of this mouth carved of the squeals
of gulls and the slow ravage of a faraway country
wishing the death of all its stars.

Our tongues tied at a certain shore
where waves eat their own froth
and shells throw their pearls.

You dig your military claws
on my hip as if to break the bird
by her wings and have her beak
always stuck within
in search of fruits and bees
that your wild trunk hosts for me.

I ask to hold me gentle
and let the sailors row through
this deep trench of longing

but you, regardless
chew my tongue like a cannibal
eating a red, fleshy berry.

OFFER

You can push me hard against my color
and then kneel in praise of the waves that sometimes
throw you away, sometimes wrap in dismay.

At my altar, you may lay a spread of exotic
wounds from forests far away, lay a batter
of dreams crushed with pine fruits and honey

You can push me gentle and blow the light
of your lungs into my bones and have my body
illuminate, so that in such light, you can
praise the nerves of our garden ecstasies.

At my altar, you may lay a spread
of embers, coins of stardust and other
cosmic emissions you gathered on your
evening walks along the many meteor belts.

You may do to me as you please—splay
this want and snatch the pulse and sow it
where grief has long repressed the streets.

The one red bloom, the rebel,
will be my offer to you.

THREE WOMEN

Before we fall in love
and change the Facebook status
from *Complicated* to *In Relation*,
before we share our house keys
and let our refrigerators
be vulnerable to each other's scrutiny,
before you stick your sweaty socks
in my shoes and take mine for yours,
before, before we accept
the offer of the grave seller calling us
now for the umpteenth time,

you should talk to your
mother about the beauty
of three women living together.

BENEATH THE HEM

That's disorder; a complete mess of grief and want stitched together to pull over such mesocarp that invites revolutions to free countries of their sweat glands

Lift it up and rise like a fallen hammock, so that the air beneath can enjoy a lift, can run a swift mile through your spine to the envy of returning creatures fed up

of lies that severe countries and relations and never bring the dining together; it terrifies me, this tectonic shift in belonging, the receding of a body from another

Descend, and bring that bowl of animalism to color the paling of my lips, the waning of my bones. Dance

till the bristled footwork of time realizes this is when we should be left alone, to redo parts that left us asking.

WHO YOU SLEEP WITH

It isn't the sexiest thing to do at thirty that you still need to sleep by your mom when a man should be counting the moles on your body, do necessary cheatings, and leave you open to his wrongful entry. But, I am so convinced you know? Convinced about this deadlock, that time at its exit, has locked me from outside and I am groping for those beautiful sun and moon taking to the stage after the wild nights of owls and street animals, comparing the data of conversions; from abundance to singularity of people like me who see men as trees hanging upside down, ringing in the air for a while before a story of theirs, knocks them down. I also fear the death of me while asleep; hear it from a wasp often mistaking my body for a hive, and dreams for nectarines. It does buzz aloud so to keep me awake and envy how the earth changes from its nightsuit to the morning... in the presence of men gathered in deep sleep. I fear exposure, you know? I don't want the darkness within to be felt by the light that shows you way to your lost belongings. So, I tuck myself in my mother's presence, feel the moving back, the receding into her womb and feel safe like a rabbit that believes she is the center of innocence and the rest are all dead within.

END MEANS

Not here, not through these sagging memories of time
that keeps gathering dust and builds castles on them

that house emptiness such as never drawn by painters
or imagined by a mind-reading-AI, or even your
nimble fingers

that promise to draw a canal connecting God to our
end means of making love like two toy birds so
mechanical...

But I understand bodies can't have it easy, bodies must
tear, must break, must kneel, and pray, bodies must
dawn

after the moon has licked up the landscape with her
fervent tongue, the way your tongue snowboards over
my Alps.

CRITICAL ACCLAIM FOR LINDA ASHOK

Whimsical and full of fierce belief. —Tishani Doshi

Linda's collection *whorelight* seeks to articulate a language for absence. Using recurring motifs of birds, worms, gardens, flowers, moths and butterflies to conjure the violence and delicacy of broken-heartedness... Each poem captures a memory. Each memory is an allegorical construction—specifically defining different manifestations of sorrow—like loss, and guilt. Here, the seeming idyllic botanical imagery is undercut by a brutal plain honesty where the ordinary reality is a love story of grief. In these poems, absence is portrayed as a childless woman and/or an absentee father. In these poems, a birthday song becomes a new tulip, the air is dank with sorrow, the garden smells like a cemetery, a neighbor grieving for his sister pulls flower vases from his lungs to capture mist. Linda's poems subtly unpicks, whilst interrogating the wounds that fester to construct lyrical emotional poetic portraits. —Malika Booker

ACKNOWLEDGEMENTS

Heartfelt gratitude to the editors and staff of the following publications for publishing/the offer to publish some of the poems that appear in this book.

"When You Talk About A Dead Deer" and "Promises We Make" (*Crab Orchard Review*), "Portrait Of Guilt and Gift" (*McNeese Review*), "Letter To The Bunion Toe Man" and "Of Waters And Manners" (*Mascara Literary Review*), "Becoming A Rice Pot" (*The Common*), "The Unmaking Of An Astronaut" (*Dirty Chai*), "Dirty Love" (*Expound*), "Chandrani" and "The Glass Kids of Firozabad" (*Noble/Gas Quarterly*), "Blood Paisleys" and "Early Lessons In Violence" (*CITY*), "Hymn For The Man By Periyar" (*Visual Verse*).

"Dirty Love" was nominated for *Best of the Net* by *Expound* in 2016 and "Chandrani" was nominated for *Best of the Net* by *Noble/ Gas Quarterly* in 2017. A lot many poems that appear here were begun and/or completed during my three-month residency at the University of Chichester, UK, as a Charles Wallace India Trust Fellow in early 2017.

It rarely happens that the poet who you so deeply admire, you get to meet him in person via a poetry fellowship and then explain to him what *whorelight* (written between 2014-2017) is all about, following with his generous inputs and then a foreword. George Szirtes. Thank you for being the inspiration you are.

Metta Sama, thank you for the recognition in the 2015 #ActualAsianPoet coverage in Literary Hub, and also for introducing me to Malika Booker. It was serendipitous to receive a timely response from her to an FB post talking about my return to Chichester from Southbank followed by an invitation to attend her performance at Apples & Snakes at Rich Mix, London. I could never imagine being at the poet's most private attic, eating Caribbean food, and listening to beautiful stories of her growing up in poetry.

Back in India, I am thankful to Tishani Doshi for her time and kind words.

Jon Tribble, thank you for being an early mentor. Alvin Pang, thank you for your company in writing numerous poems that appear here. N Ravi Shankeran (RaSh), you know how Meena Kandasamy and I are forever grateful to you for putting us together with our poems. Thanks to Saddiq Dzukogi for the rigour of his heart, for bearing me, to Vinita Agrawal, for reading many of these poems, for editing them, and whispering unto them, *you pretty ones…*

Thanks to dad for reasons and mum for lessons in restraint. Donnie, I knew you were born five years younger to me until late that your maturity proved it otherwise.

Last but not the least, gratitude to the missing ones…